THE ANTI COLORING BOOK of Masterpieces ®

Susan Striker

AN OWL BOOK
Henry Holt and Company   New York

To Jill and Robbie

"To create forms means to live. Are not the children who construct directly from the secrets of their emotions more creative than the imitators of Greek form?"

—August Macke

Henry Holt and Company, Inc.
Publishers since 1866
115 West 18th Street
New York, New York 10011

Henry Holt ® is a registered trademark
of Henry Holt and Company, Inc.

Published in Canada by Fitzhenry & Whiteside Ltd.,
195 Allstate Parkway, Markham, Ontario L3R 4T8.

ISBN 0-8050-2644-4 (An Owl Book: pbk.)

Henry Holt books are available for special promotions
and premiums. For details contact:
Director, Special Markets.

Printed in the United States of America
All first editions are printed on acid-free paper.∞
10 9 8 7 6 5 4 3

Many thanks to Mary Doherty, Miranda Haydn, and Anita Duquette for their
invaluable assistance.

Grateful acknowledgment is made for use of the following:
"The Great Figure" from *Collected Earlier Poems of William Carlos Williams*.
Copyright 1938 by New Directions Publishing Corporation. Reprinted by
permission of New Directions.

Introduction

In art, there is rarely a "right" or "wrong." The artist makes choices based on mood, available materials, and personal preference. Should the color be blue or green? Should the shape be oval or round? Should the portrait show the subject smiling or not? How should objects be arranged? Each decision an artist makes determines how the finished work will look.

What if some of the decisions were different? What if *you* could decide how a masterpiece would be completed, instead of the artist who actually painted it? How would your own taste, your choices, your mood affect the way it turned out? *The Anti–Coloring Book of Masterpieces* gives you a chance to find out. It includes 38 works of art—some thousands of years old, some very recent—with part of the original missing from each one, for you to fill in.

Artists have traditionally looked to the old masters for inspiration. Sometimes an artist will copy a masterpiece exactly, to learn more about how it was painted; or an artist might pay respect to an older masterpiece by using the same subject and arrangement of objects, but painting in his or her own personal style; or occasionally one artist may parody another's painting. Great works of art give us something to think about. They inspire us to see the world from a new perspective.

Every work of art is a personal statement by the artist. You and the original artist will bring different backgrounds, experience, and materials to a work of art. It is clear from the example below, for instance, that the painter Paul Cézanne and eleven-year-old John Mengel—who had never seen the completed original before starting on his own imaginary visit to a clockmaker's home—had different ideas about how the interior should look. Perhaps if Cézanne had had magic markers his palette would also have been brighter.

In using this book, please do not look at how the original work was completed until you have finished your drawing as you want to. Remember this:

YOU ARE THE ARTIST

Whatever you draw or paint with enthusiasm, with freedom to express yourself without fear of ridicule, makes you the equal of any other great artist.

This book is intended primarily to stimulate the imagination of young artists. While working with my students on some of these pages, however, I was delighted to discover an unintended bonus. Children became very curious about whatever work of art they were completing. They began asking questions about the artist, expressed strong opinions about how the original work compared to their own, and, I later found out, did additional research in the public library. One boy proudly brought art books to school to show me how much better his picture was than the original by "that weirdo Dali."

It is my hope, then, that this book will not only foster creativity and expose budding artists of all ages to a variety of styles and periods, but also open a door to the wonder and endless richness of art history.

Lightly Touching uses geometric shapes to express the artist's emotions. How would you finish it to show your feelings?

Picasso painted The Charnel House because he was upset by what he read in the newspaper. Has any event made you want to draw?

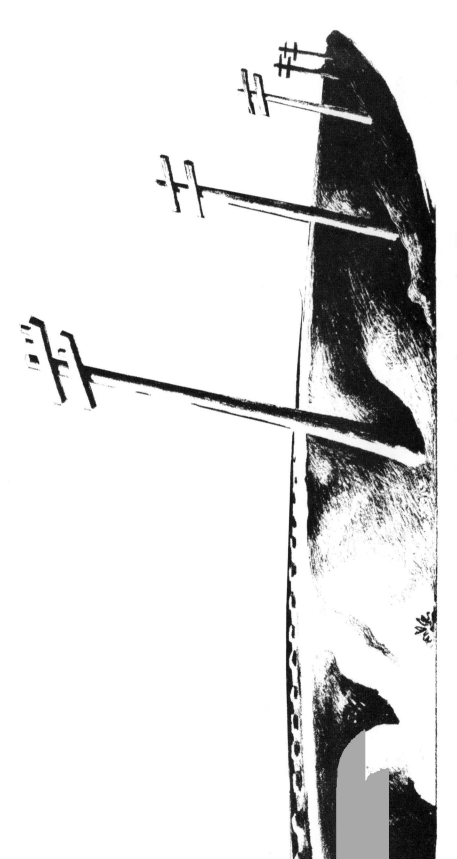

A train comes along this track once a day. Here it comes now!

Sometimes it can be fun to work so quickly you don't think about the final results until you've finished.

The artist who did Free Form *dripped and splashed paint all over the canvas. Let loose and have fun!*

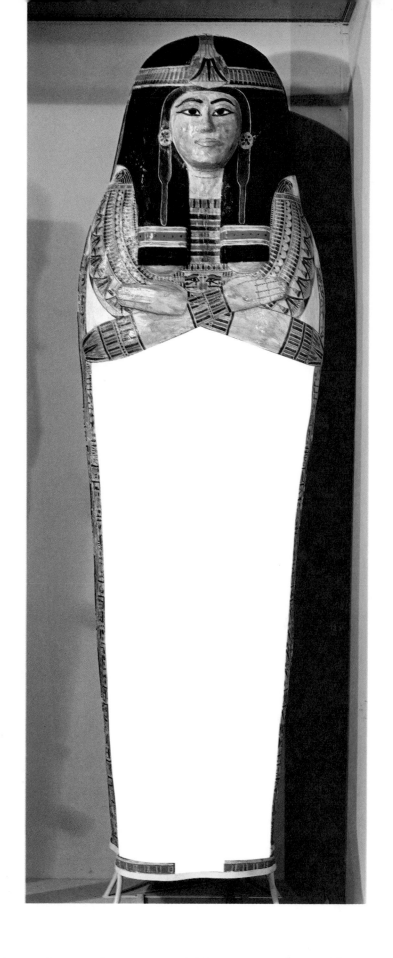

How would you have decorated Henttowe's coffin if you were
a priest in ancient Egypt?

de sco nicholao. anf.   b: se amabilem exhibut.

Anctus dei nicho   Ra pro nobis beat
laus pontifica   brate nicholae. Rin.
ll decoratus in sua omit Ut digni efficiamur

A raging storm at sea illustrated this manuscript page
from a prayer book.

This woman is famous for her mysterious smile.

Velázquez painted his daughter busy at work. What do you think she was creating?

What is the wise Greek philosopher Aristotle thinking about?

What would be interesting enough to make this man look up from his book?

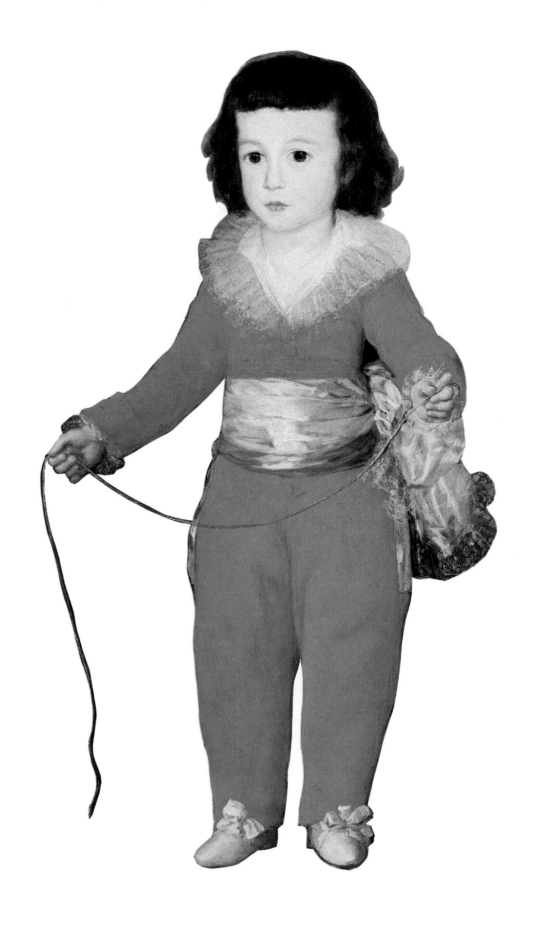

This is a picture of a young boy with all his pets.

What is on the other side of these bars?

Provide Degas' ballerinas with a stage set.

If Cézanne's father were reading a newspaper written and illustrated by you, how would this painting look?

Madame Charpentier is relaxing with her family in their home.

What do you imagine is happening while the gypsy sleeps?

This is Mary Cassatt's sister Lydia at the garden in their summer home.
What do you think she is knitting?

Would you like to use binoculars to see a close-up view of an exciting event?

Van Gogh painted this portrait against a background of wallpaper.

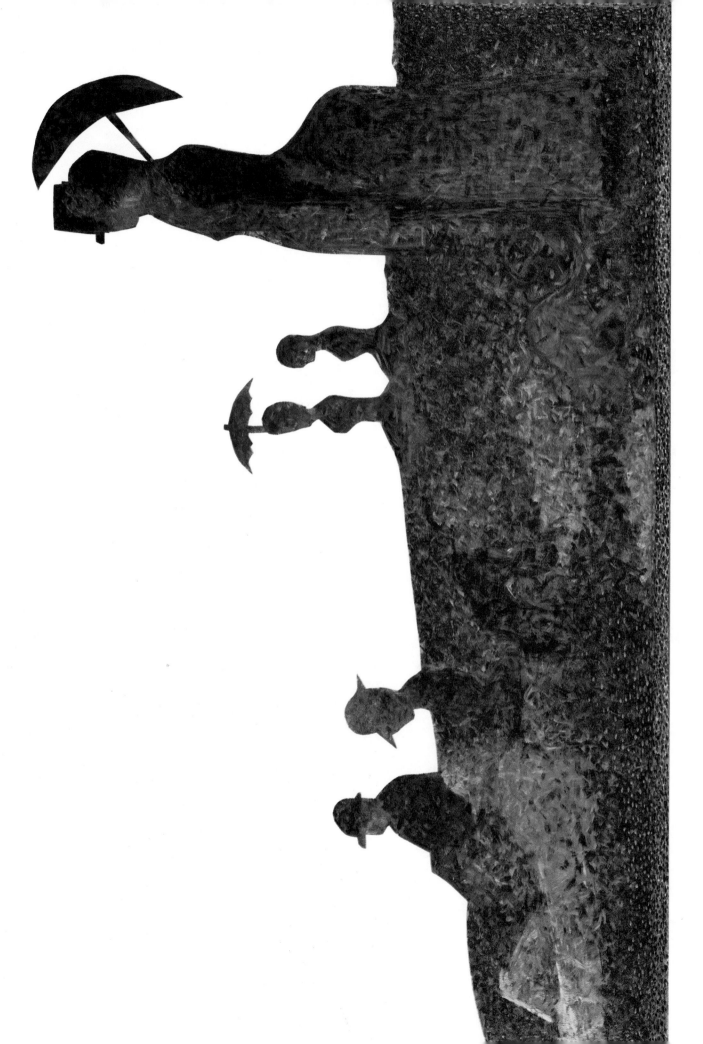

These people are watching everyone spend an afternoon in the park.

What is outside the window of Bonnard's *Breakfast Room*?

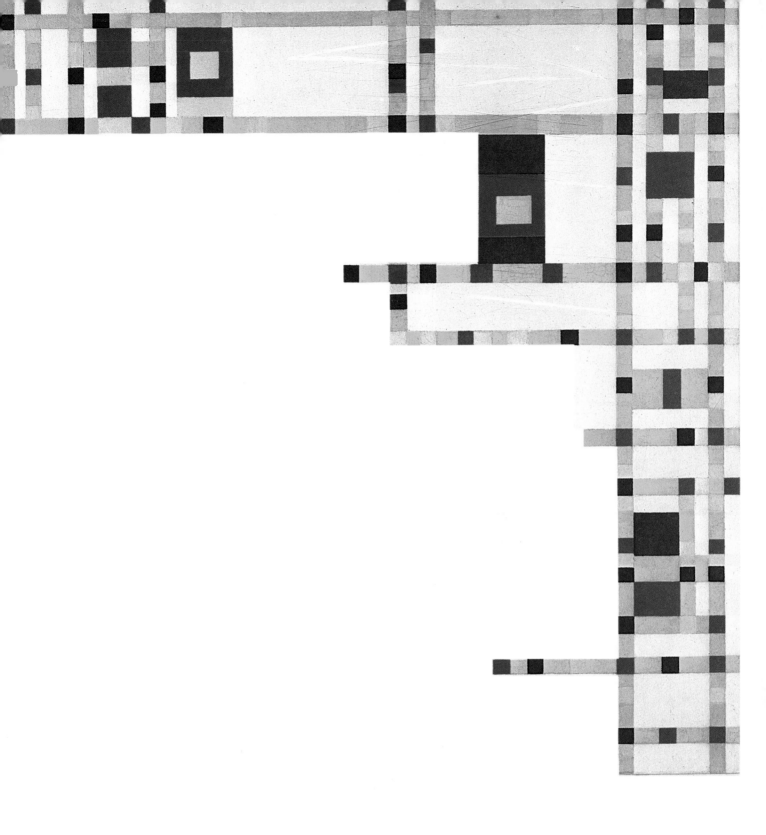

Do the shapes and colors in *Broadway Boogie Woogie* remind you of jazz?

What do you think this woman sees when she looks in the mirror?

The subject of this painting is a number. What number is it, and what do you think the rest of the picture should look like?

Who or what else is in the barnyard with Milton Avery's White Rooster?

Can you imagine why Pavel Tchelitchew called
this painting *Hide-and-Seek*?

These are two panels in a three-part painting about the machine age by Roy Lichtenstein. How would you fill in the missing panel?

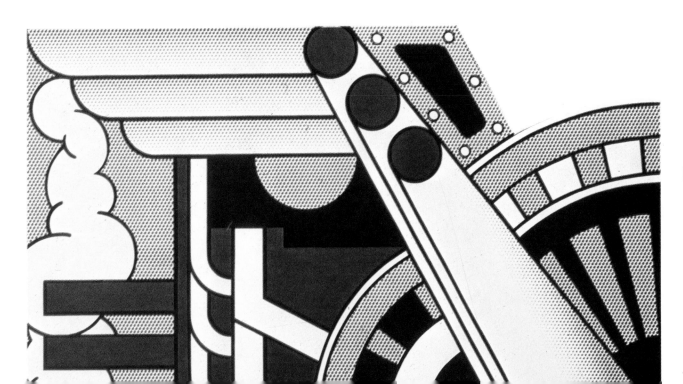

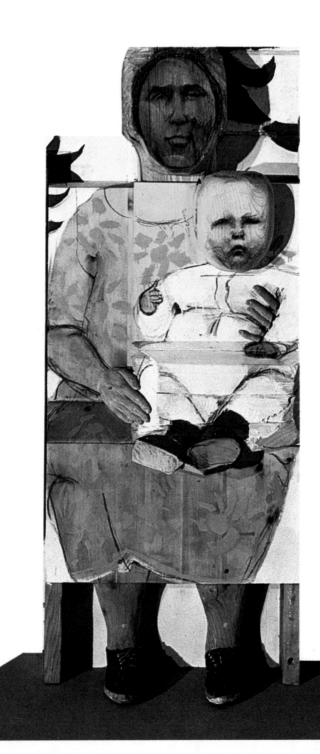

If these are the mother and baby in Marisol's assemblage *Family,*
what do you think the rest of the group looks like?

The picture on this vase shows athletes practicing.

*This **City of Ambition** is seen through the creative lens of Alfred Stieglitz's camera.*

Where are the horses taking this man on a cold, dreary November evening?

This is Calder's playful idea of what a person can look like.

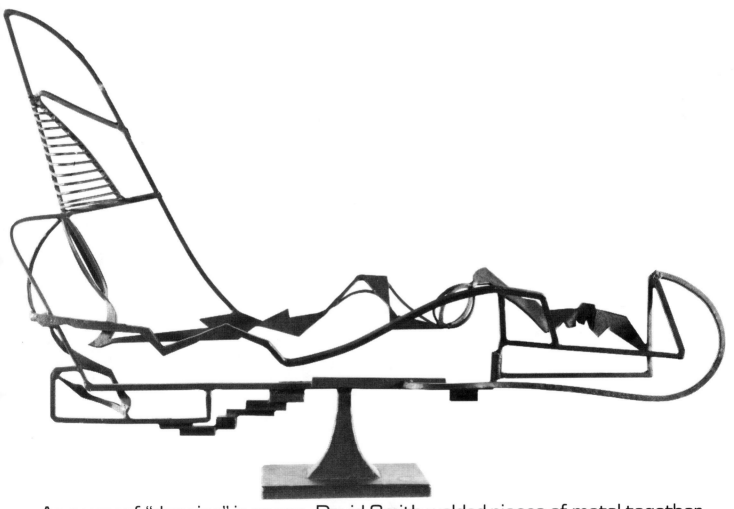

As a way of "drawing" in space, David Smith welded pieces of metal together to create *Hudson River Landscape*.

You can complete a collage by pasting paper and other materials onto the background. How would you finish Marca-Relli's collage?

Can you just imagine what the rest of the team looks like?

Bridget Riley's *Current* is inspired by wave patterns on the water and can play tricks on your eyes.

About the Masterpieces

WASSILY KANDINSKY. *Lightly Touching.* 1931.
Oil on cardboard, 27⅝ × 19¼″.
The Sidney and Harriet Janis Collection.
Gift to The Museum of Modern Art, New York.

Wassily Kandinsky (1866–1944), one of the originators of abstract art, felt that art must express something of the artist's personality. Born in Moscow, he helped found the Academy of Arts and Sciences there in 1921. The following year he went to Germany and worked at the famous Bauhaus, an influential school that experimented with abstract and modern art and architecture, becoming its president for a year. When his art was condemned by the Nazis as "degenerate," he fled to Paris.

Lightly Touching is typical of Kandinsky's Bauhaus period, which lasted from 1922 to 1932. During that time he concentrated on the theme of the circle, square, and triangle. In this picture, tension is created by the fact that only the edges of the shapes in the painting touch. No shapes overlap or fit together.

PABLO PICASSO. *The Charnel House.* 1944–45.
Oil and charcoal on canvas, 6′ 6⅝″ × 9′ 2½″.
Collection. The Museum of Modern Art, New York.
Acquired through the Mrs. Sam A. Lewisohn
Bequest, Mrs. Marya Bernard in memory
of her husband, Dr. D. Bernard, and
anonymous funds.

Most of Pablo Ruiz y Picasso's (1881–1973) paintings were inspired by his personal experience, but *The Charnel House*, like his famous *Guernica*, is an exception. Both paintings were reactions to the horrors of war.

Picasso did this painting after viewing newspaper photographs of concentration camps in 1944. Like the photographs, the painting is done entirely in black and white. It shows a pile of dead bodies in a room that also contains a table with food on it. In the pile of bodies one can find the figures of a man, woman, and child. The man's hands are tied behind his back like an animal about to be slaughtered. The people are wounded and suffering, while the meal on the table suggests that someone may uncaringly sit down to eat, back turned on the suffering of the victims. Flames in the upper-right-hand corner remind us of the people who died by fire in the crematoriums of the concentration camps during World War II.

THOMAS HART BENTON. *Express Train.* 1924.
Lithograph, 12¹¹/₁₆ × 23¼".
Collection of The Whitney Museum of
American Art, New York.
Photograph by Geoffrey Clements.

Thomas Hart Benton (1889–1975) was born in Neosho, Missouri. His father was a congressman. When he was a child, Benton loved drawing Indians and trains.

He worked as a draftsman and painted scenes showing daily life in America. Because his paintings reflected his rural background in a small American town, he was considered a "regionalist" painter. Benton's work was inspired by history, folklore, and the everyday lives of common people.

FRANZ KLINE. *Painting Number 2.* 1954.
Oil on canvas, 6' 8½" × 8' 9".
Collection, The Museum of Modern Art, New York.
Mr. and Mrs. Joseph H. Hazen and
Mr. and Mrs. Francis F. Rosenbaum funds.

Along with Jackson Pollock and Willem de Kooning, Franz Kline (1910–1962) was a leading Abstract Expressionist painter. These artists used the physical act of painting to express their personal feelings. The most significant and influential style to emerge from the 1940s and 1950s, Abstract Expressionism was the first major breakthrough in painting to originate in the United States. With its development, the center of the art world moved from Paris to New York.

Franz Kline's most important paintings were quite large, and after 1950 he painted almost everything entirely in black and white. Although *Painting Number 2* appears to be completely spontaneous, Kline usually made many sketches before doing a painting. He executed the paintings themselves very quickly. Some of them have been compared to oriental calligraphy. Of his characteristic black images on white canvas he said: "I kept simplifying the forms in black and white and breaking down the structure into essential elements." Kline disagreed with critics who said his works relied on their emotional impact. When he died at the height of his career, he left the world a legacy of many paintings which were, by his own standards, great "whether or not the painter's emotion comes across."

JACKSON POLLOCK. *Free Form.* 1946.
Oil on canvas, 19¼ × 14".
The Sidney and Harriet Janis Collection. Gift to
The Museum of Modern Art, New York.

Jackson Pollock (1912–1956) stopped doing realistic paintings in 1945 and developed Action Painting, which depended on his subconscious. Tacking canvases as large as twenty feet wide onto the floor, and working in a kind of rhythmic frenzy, Pollock threw, splashed, and dripped enamel and aluminum paints. He said:

> This way I can walk around it, work from the four sides and literally be *in* the painting. . . . When I am *in* my painting, I'm not aware of what I'm doing. It is only after a sort of "get acquainted" period that I see what I have been about. I have no fears about making changes, destroying the image, etc., because the painting has a life of its own. I try to let it come through.

Although imitated by many lesser artists and ridiculed by the public, Pollock brought to his work a wildness and freedom, yet he never lost control of it. This combination produced the fluid lines that are instantly recognizable as his. Pollock became one of the most important and influential Abstract Expressionists.

Outer and inner coffin of Henttowe.
Wood. From Thebes, Deir al-Bahri.
The Metropolitan Museum of Art, New York.
Museum Excavations, 1923–24.
Rogers Fund, 1925.

Queen Pharaoh Henttowe was only twenty-one years old when she died during the Twenty-first Dynasty (1085–950 B.C.) in ancient Egypt. She was buried in a tomb that had originally held another coffin but was plundered. Wrapped in linen and holding personal possessions such as jewelry, Henttowe was buried in this wooden coffin decorated with paint, gold, and semiprecious stones. The coffin was discovered at Deir al-Bahri, Egypt, where other ancient artifacts of high quality have been found. The fine artwork being done during the time of Henttowe included gold masks, silver coffins, jewels, and utensils used in royal and aristocratic burials.

POL, JEAN, and HERMAN DE LIMBOURG. *The Belles Heures of Jean, Duke of Berry.*
Folio 168: "St. Nicholas Stops the Storm at Sea."
c. 1406–09. Ink, tempera, and gold leaf on parchment, 9⅜" × 6⅝".
The Metropolitan Museum of Art, New York. The Cloisters Collection, purchase, 1954.

This medieval book of hours is a private prayer book illustrated in the early fifteenth century by three brothers, Pol, Jean, and Herman de Limbourg. The work was commissioned by Jean d'Evreaux, Duke of Berry, whose family was noted for its interest in art and who provided the brothers with financial security, a creative work environment, and the encouragement to be original. Such books got their name from the fact that the prayers in them were arranged according to the seven hours of the day when they were to be recited by the worshiper. This book of hours is considered by many to be the greatest example of the courtly art of France. Its drawings are excellent and the decorations are unusual and exciting.

Folio 168 shows Nicholas, Bishop of Myra and patron saint of sailors, who was famous during his lifetime for suddenly appearing when people needed help. Although it was uncommon to represent wind and stormy weather in paintings of this period, here a boat caught in a storm is about to capsize. The passengers appear to have given up hope; they do not yet know that St. Nicholas is about to rescue them.

LEONARDO DA VINCI. *Mona Lisa (La Giaconda)*. c. 1503–05.
Oil on poplar panel, 30¼ × 20⅞".
The Louvre, Paris. Photograph Musées Nationaux.

Leonardo da Vinci (1452–1519) was the ultimate Renaissance man. He was a modern thinker who did not live by tradition or superstition but by observation and experience.

At the age of thirteen Leonardo was apprenticed to the artist Verrocchio, with whom he studied painting, sculpture, goldsmithing, and draftsmanship. An accomplished musician, poet, architect, and engineer, he carried out scientific experiments in anatomy, geology, botany, and other fields in order to become a better painter. His most important contribution to painting was his work with chiaroscuro, the use of dark shadows and strongly contrasting light to express a mood dramatically.

Leonardo was a great intellectual who felt that painting should not be merely decorative. *Mona Lisa* is an example of the way he encouraged viewers to think about as well as look at his work. Mona Lisa's smile has made the painting one of the most famous in the world. The viewer can interpret her expression many different ways. One is always tempted to return to it and ponder.

DIEGO VELAZQUEZ. *The Needlewoman*. c. 1640.
Oil on canvas, 29⅛ × 23⅝".
The National Gallery of Art, Washington, D.C. Andrew Mellon Collection, 1937.

The Needlewoman by Diego Rodríguez de Silva y Velázquez (1599–1660) is a portrait of his daughter, Francesca, engaged in the humble activity of sewing. It is an unusual subject for Velázquez, since most of his artwork had either a religious or a classical theme. The silvery light is typical of Velázquez's work, and the composition is arranged to emphasize the woman's busy hands.

Velázquez's portraits are noted for their great insight into the sitter's personality. He and Goya are considered the greatest Spanish portraitists of all time.

REMBRANDT HARMENSZ VAN RYN. *Aristotle with a Bust of Homer.* 1653.
Oil on canvas, 56½ × 53¾".
The Metropolitan Museum of Art, New York.
Purchased with the special funds and gifts of friends of the museum, 1961.

Dutch Baroque painting, with its meticulous details and delightful subjects, might be considered merely charming if it were not for the grandeur brought to it by the work of Rembrandt van Ryn. Rembrandt painted with the precision required by the times, but his genius at arranging space, portraying three dimensions, and using light dramatically set him apart from his contemporaries. His work involves its viewers personally and evokes strong emotions.

Rembrandt was misunderstood in his lifetime (1606–1669), alternately famous and ignored. He lost his home and collection of paintings when he was declared bankrupt in 1656. Now he is probably the most widely admired old master.

Between 1652 and 1663 Rembrandt did three paintings of great people of the world. In addition to *Aristotle with a Bust of Homer,* symbolizing poetry, he also painted *Alexander the Great* (representing philosophy) and *Homer Instructing Two of His Followers* (symbolizing poetry). Rembrandt dressed Aristotle in a gold costume rather than in authentic robes of the period, probably because he preferred the costume he saw in his imagination to one that would have been historically correct. Aristotle's sleeves are bathed in light, and they direct attention to the most important features of the painting: Aristotle's thoughtful face and the statue. All other details of the picture fade into the background.

AERT DE GELDER. *The Rest on the Flight into Egypt.* c. 1690.
Oil on canvas, 43¼ × 46½".
Courtesy, The Museum of Fine Arts, Boston.
Maria T. B. Hopkins Fund.

Aert de Gelder (1645–1727), who painted mostly biblical subjects and portraits, studied with Rembrandt in the 1660s. His scenes from the New Testament, such as *Rest on the Flight into Egypt,* are done in warm colors and have a glow and technique that make the viewer think immediately of that great Dutch master. But since the younger Gelder lived nearly sixty years beyond Rembrandt's death, his work also reflects later styles, such as Rococo, and his colors are slightly lighter.

FRANCISCO DE GOYA. *Don Manuel Osorio de Zuñiga.* c. late 1780s.
Oil on canvas, 50 × 40".
The Metropolitan Museum of Art, New York.
Jules S. Bache Collection, 1949.

Francisco José de Goya y Lucientes (1746–1828) was born in Spain but lived the last years of his life in France. As was the custom during these times, Goya decided on his life's career by the time he was fourteen and was apprenticed to an artist to study painting and assist the artist in his studio.

Goya is considered one of the most important portrait painters in the history of art, and he is also noted for his studies exploring violence and savagery in human beings.

This portrait by Goya is of four-year-old Don Manuel Osorio de Zuñiga. The child is shown wearing red trousers, a white frilled collar, and white shoes. He is holding a string tied to a bird. In the bird's beak is an engraved card which also shows the artist's signature. With Don Manuel are three cats and a birdcage containing several small birds.

EDOUARD MANET. *Gare St.-Lazare.* 1873.
Oil on canvas, 36¾ × 45⅛".
The National Gallery of Art, Washington, D.C.
Gift of Horace Havemeyer in memory of his mother, Louisine W. Havemeyer.

Edouard Manet (1832–1883) was born in France to a conservative, wealthy family who opposed his choice of a career as an artist. But his father finally let him attend the Ecole des Beaux-Arts and helped support him.

Manet studied with Thomas Couture and learned a great deal about handling tones from his teacher, who objected to his free style of painting. After leaving Couture's studio, he painted *Déjeuner sur l'Herbe (Luncheon on the Grass)* and *Olympia.* Both of these pictures were based on classic Renaissance paintings, yet the way Manet treated them, combining boldly staring nude women with clothed models, scandalized people at the time.

Manet's free brushwork, flat forms, strong contrast of light and dark, and fresh new interpretation of the old masters paved the way for the Impressionist style of painting that dominated the art world through the late nineteenth and early twentieth centuries.

EDGAR DEGAS. *The Curtain Call (Danseuse au bouquet, saluant sur la scène).* c. 1877.
Pastel, 29½ × 30¾″.
The Louvre, Musée de l'Impressionnisme, Paris.

Hilaire Germain Edgar Degas (1834–1917) was a French Impressionist whose favorite subjects were dancers and racehorses. He began painting ballet dancers in 1873 and the following year showed his work in the First Impressionist Exhibition. Critics ridiculed his paintings—as well as those of other Impressionists—and the public was hostile. But since Degas had a private income, he did not have to depend on popularity to continue painting.

Degas wrote, "Drawing is not what one sees, but what one must make others see." He made his viewers see the beauty of women posed naturally in fleeting moments—while bathing, working, dressing, or relaxing. His arrangements are asymmetrical; most of his subjects are shown from an unusual viewpoint. In *The Curtain Call*, the light cast upward on the curtseying dancer's face, the casual clusters of dancers in the background with their attention directed to the side, and the sketchy partial figure of the dancer walking onstage (far left) all contribute to a feeling of naturalness, of one brief instant captured in its informal beauty.

PAUL CEZANNE. *The Artist's Father.* 1886.
Oil on canvas, 78⅛ × 47″.
The National Gallery of Art, Washington, D.C.
Collection of Mr. and Mrs. Paul Mellon.

Paul Cézanne (1839–1906) was a French painter important in the Impressionist movement. He was particularly interested in the essential geometric forms of things he painted, and his later work became increasingly abstract. In fact, his paintings had a great influence on the development of Cubism.

One subject Cézanne liked to paint was his father, who posed for three paintings and many drawings. They had a difficult relationship but the elder Cézanne supported his son, even though he did not understand Paul's work. The father owned a bank, where he wanted Paul to work, but Paul was very unhappy there and thought only of painting. Finally his father gave him an allowance so that he could continue working in the field of art.

In *The Artist's Father*, Cézanne has painted the subject in a way that makes him look very solid and sturdy, almost like a sculpture. Although his large, weighty form suggests the father figure and impressive bank president, his posture and expression betray the artist's tenderness, which did not always show when they were together.

PIERRE AUGUSTE RENOIR. *Madame Charpentier and Her Children.* 1878.
Oil on canvas. 60½ × 74⅞".
The Metropolitan Museum of Art, New York.
Wolfe Fund, 1907.
Catharine Lorillard Wolfe Collection.

Pierre Auguste Renoir (1841–1919) showed artistic talent as a youngster and was apprenticed to a porcelain manufacturer, for whom he decorated plates. He later studied at the Ecole de Beaux-Arts in Paris, where he met artists Claude Monet, Frédéric Bazille, and Alfred Sisley. He and his fellow artists, called Impressionists, explored the effects of changing light on a subject and painted outdoors rather than in a studio. Renoir's paintings were done in a lively, lyrical style, and he used bright colors and free brushstrokes.

Madame Charpentier and Her Children was a great opportunity for Renoir to publicize his work. Madame Charpentier was well known in intellectual circles in Paris, and, to please her, when the painting was exhibited in the Salon the following year, it was hung in an important spot.

The picture shows Madame Charpentier seated in her luxurious home and wearing a gown by Worth, a leading dress designer of the time. Renoir painted the gown as well as other parts of the picture in black, which he considered "the queen of colors." The child sitting on the sofa is a three-year-old boy—not a girl, as many people think. His name was Paul, and he died at the age of twenty in a war. Georgette, the little girl on the dog's back, was six years old.

HENRI ROUSSEAU. *The Sleeping Gypsy.* 1897.
Oil on canvas, 51 × 79".
Collection, The Museum of Modern Art, New York.
Gift of Mrs. Simon Guggenheim.

Henri Julien Félix Rousseau (1844–1910) began painting when he was about forty years old, even while he contined to work full-time as a French customs officer. Although he never formally studied art, he copied old masters in the Louvre museum and was a friend of many artists, such as Robert Delaunay, Maurice Vlaminck, Paul Gauguin, and Pablo Picasso.

The Sleeping Gypsy, one of his best-known works, depicts a frightening dream. Rousseau is called a "primitive" painter because of the simplicity of his style, but his skillful paintings indicate that he was not ignorant of many of the principles of fine arts despite his lack of formal education in that field.

MARY CASSATT. *Lydia Crocheting in the Garden at Marly.* 1880.
Oil on canvas, 26 × 37″.
The Metropolitan Museum of Art, New York. Gift of Mrs. Gardner Cassatt, 1965.

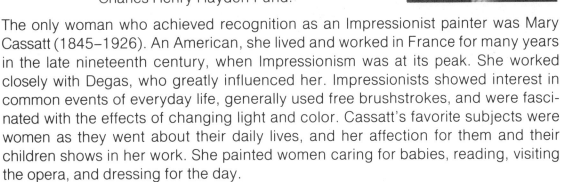

MARY CASSATT. *At the Opera.* 1879.
Oil on canvas, 31½ × 25½″.
Courtesy, The Museum of Fine Arts, Boston. Charles Henry Hayden Fund.

The only woman who achieved recognition as an Impressionist painter was Mary Cassatt (1845–1926). An American, she lived and worked in France for many years in the late nineteenth century, when Impressionism was at its peak. She worked closely with Degas, who greatly influenced her. Impressionists showed interest in common events of everyday life, generally used free brushstrokes, and were fascinated with the effects of changing light and color. Cassatt's favorite subjects were women as they went about their daily lives, and her affection for them and their children shows in her work. She painted women caring for babies, reading, visiting the opera, and dressing for the day.

Lydia Crocheting in the Garden at Marly is in keeping with Cassatt's interest in this subject. It portrays her sister sitting in the garden of their summer home. *At the Opera* is one of many paintings she did of an opera setting. Both pictures show Cassatt's free brushstroke, an interesting composition with strong diagonals that pull the viewer's attention to the main subject, and the overall softness of her art.

VINCENT VAN GOGH. *La Berceuse* (or *Woman Rocking a Cradle*). 1888–89.
Oil on canvas, 36¼ × 28¾″.
Collection, State Museum Kröller-Müller, Otterlo, The Netherlands.

Vincent van Gogh (1853–1890) painted *La Berceuse* (or *Woman Rocking a Cradle*) in 1888–89. It is one of many portraits he did of Madame Roulin, the wife of his friend the postman. In three months in 1889 he painted her five times.

The subject is fat, has orange hair, and wears a bright green dress that contrasts strongly with the red chair she is sitting in. The yellow cord of a cradle she is holding in her hands emphasizes the strong attachment between a mother and her child. In fact, the sitter may have symbolized motherhood to van Gogh. The horizon line lies on two different levels, and reminds one of the rocking of the cradle.

As an Expressionist painter, van Gogh projected his own feelings into his paintings of objects, people, and landscapes. He painted in bright, pure colors and used strong color contrasts to evoke emotional responses from the viewer.

Van Gogh shot himself fatally while in a mental asylum, and it is easy to see how troubled he was by studying his later paintings. He did revealing portraits and self-portraits, still-lifes, and powerful, vibrant landscapes. His work had a great influence on painters in the twentieth century, and the tragic story of his life and death has captured the imagination of many people.

GEORGES SEURAT. *A Sunday Afternoon at the Grande Jatte.* c. 1884.
Oil on canvas, 27⅞ × 41⅛".
The Metropolitan Museum of Art, New York.
Bequest of Samuel A. Lewisohn, 1951.

Georges Seurat (1859–1891), a French painter, had an extremely intellectual approach to his art and made scientific studies of the effects of color and light on the eye. The way he painted was methodical and painstaking. He applied color to a canvas in small, round dots of equal size. He chose color combinations scientifically based upon the effects they had on each other and the impression they made on the eye. Close up, his paintings seem to be individual colored dots, but the human eye mixes the dots and the viewer sees the right colors and shapes of objects when standing farther away from the painting.

This painting of *A Sunday Afternoon at the Grande Jatte* is a preliminary sketch he made before finishing the final, larger version that now hangs in the Art Institute of Chicago. The Grande Jatte is an island near a suburb of Paris where the people of Paris go on summer weekends to fish, row boats, and relax along the Seine River.

PIERRE BONNARD. *The Breakfast Room.* c. 1930–31.
Oil on canvas, 62⅞ × 44⅞".
Collection, The Museum of Modern Art, New York.
Given anonymously.

This interior by Pierre Bonnard (1867–1947), with blue and pink patterned wallpaper, various bright objects, and purple shadows, is alive with color. *The Breakfast Room* was done with short brushstrokes to show the shimmery effect of the light. The composition is symmetrical, which was unusual for this period, and the diagonal lines of the tablecloth and curtains lead one's attention to the view beyond the window. This intimate look at an interior has a sense of privacy and warmth that illustrates why the style of painting used by Bonnard was called Intimist.

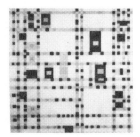

PIET MONDRIAN. *Broadway Boogie Woogie.* 1942–43.
Oil on canvas, 50 × 50".
Collection, The Museum of Modern Art, New York.
Given anonymously.

In 1917 Piet Mondrian (1872–1944) helped found the De Stijl movement of painters and architects in Holland. These painters emphasized clarity and order in their art by using straight lines, right angles, and primary colors (red, yellow, and blue). Their work symbolized human dominance over the random forms of nature.

Broadway Boogie Woogie, Mondrian's last painting, was unfinished when he died. It is complicated and vibrant; its colors and lines seem to move on the canvas, reflecting the fast pace of American urban life. Mondrian used adhesive tape to block out his composition and help him keep his lines straight, and some pieces of tape remain on the painting.

PABLO PICASSO. *Girl Before a Mirror.* 1932.
Oil on canvas, 64 × 51¼".
Collection, The Museum of Modern Art, New York. Gift of
Mrs. Simon Guggenheim.

Pablo Ruiz y Picasso (1881–1973) was enormously talented and extremely hard-working, and he had a very powerful personality. This rare combination made him the most important and influential artist of the twentieth century. He achieved more popular acclaim and wealth in his lifetime than any other artist ever has. He worked in many different styles and media and originated much of what is unique about this century's art. Many important artists are indebted to him for his influence on their work.

With its bright colors and strongly outlined geometric shapes, *Girl Before a Mirror* looks like stained glass. It is a portrait of a young woman named Marie-Thérèse Wilter. Picasso's love for Marie-Thérèse marked a turning point in his style. After he met her, he began painting in livelier colors, using more full, rounded shapes than he had earlier. Here, the subject's beauty shows in half the painting, but her image in the mirror changes to something ugly. The style of the mirror is called, in French, *psyche*, which is also the Greek word for "soul." Picasso may have intended this painting to represent a popular superstition that a mirror has magical properties and can reflect the soul of the person looking into it.

CHARLES HENRY DEMUTH. *I Saw the Figure 5 in Gold.* 1928.
Oil on composition board, 36 × 29¾".
The Metropolitan Museum of Art, New York. Alfred Stieglitz
Collection, 1949.

Born in Pennsylvania, Charles Henry Demuth (1883–1935) was one of the pioneers of the modern-art movement in the United States. His paintings—cold, geometric interpretations of the industrial world—have great strength, yet are also light and delicate. Demuth originated a style of painting known as the "poster portrait."

I Saw the Figure 5 in Gold, considered by many to be his most important painting, was inspired by a poem by William Carlos Williams, who was a close friend of his.

The Great Figure

Among the rain
and lights
I saw the figure 5
in gold
on a red
firetruck
moving
tense
unheeded
to gong clangs
siren howls
and wheels rambling
through the dark city

MILTON AVERY. *White Rooster.* 1947.
Oil on canvas, 61½ × 50¾".
The Metropolitan Museum of Art, New York. Gift of
Joyce Blaffer von Bothmer, 1975.

Milton Avery was a New Yorker who lived from 1893 to 1965. He is best known for being an important link in American art between such European color masters as Matisse and the abstract color-field painters of the 1960s, such as Mark Rothko.

During the 1940s Avery developed a style which, while abstract, always contained a recognizable subject. His works, with their large, flat areas of color, were quite different from the Social Realist style popular during that period. This barnyard scene, *White Rooster*, is typical of his art, with its soft but strong arrangements of flat, colorful shapes.

PAVEL TCHELITCHEW. *Hide-and-Seek (Cache-cache).*
1940–42.
Oil on canvas, 6' 6½" × 7' ¾".
Collection, The Museum of Modern Art, New York.
Mrs. Simon Guggenheim Fund.

Pavel Tchelitchew (pronounced Chel'-ĭ-chef) was an American painter who was born in Russia in 1898 and died in 1957. Most of his paintings showed some sort of metamorphosis—the changing of one object into another. Over eight years he did a sequence of drawings that finally became the large painting *Hide-and-Seek*. In this symbolic picture, a gnarled tree becomes the figures of children, as the artist expressed his philosophy on the mystery of life. Art historian Alfred A. Barr, Jr., said of it: "The tree of life becomes a clock of the seasons; its greens and fiery reds and wintry blues celebrate the annual cycle of death and rebirth." Each color Tchelitchew used is also symbolic. Ocher signifies the earth and bones; green stands for lymph and water; blue indicates arteries, veins, and air; and yellow with a magenta halo symbolizes nerves and fire. Even minor details have significance in his work: the dandelion signifies "ephemeral existence and terrific tenacity."

ROY LICHTENSTEIN. *Preparedness.* 1969.
Magna on canvas, three panels,
each 120 × 72".
Collection, The Solomon R. Guggenheim
Museum, New York.
Photograph by Robert E. Mates.

Roy Lichtenstein was born in New York in 1923. His early paintings were studies of the Old West. After going through a period in which he did abstract symbolic paintings, he began in 1961 to use a shading technique known as Ben Day dots, and his main subjects became advertisements and comic strips. Throughout the 1960s he was a leader in the Pop Art movement.

Lichtenstein described this work, *Preparedness*, as a "muralesque painting about our military-industrial complex" and chose the title to suggest a call to arms. It is actually three paintings hung side by side to form a triptych, with the three panels visually unified by the diagonals of the composition. Dots and bright primary colors are used in all three panels.

The panel on the left is of the smokestacks of factories. The center panel shows a hand holding a hammer and gears and a row of soldiers. In the right-hand panel we see another soldier and the window of an airplane.

MARISOL ESCOBAR. *The Family.* 1962.
Painted wood and other materials in three sections,
82⅝ × 65".
Collection, The Museum of Modern Art, New York.
Advisory Committee Fund.

Marisol Escobar (1930–   ) was born in France but has lived in New York since 1950. A sculptor, she creates works that include painting, carving, drawing, plaster casts, and objects she has collected. Her figures or groups of figures are frequently larger than life-size, and most are comments on the values of modern society. Her work, such as this sculpture titled *The Family*, combines irony, satire, pity, and humor.

Lekythos (Greek vase). Black-figured athletes practicing.
c. 525–500 B.C.
The Metropolitan Museum of Art, New York. Rogers Fund, 1906.

During the sixth century B.C., Greek vases were made of red clay and decorated with black glaze. Because they usually showed scenes of daily life or portrayed myths, they have given us much of the information we have about Greek life during the period they were made. This vase shows athletes practicing. The ornamental design framing the scene divides the vase and decorates the areas not covered by the scene. The lotus flower and palmette in the borders were favorite decorations of the period.

ALFRED STIEGLITZ. *City of Ambition.* 1911.
Photograph.
The Metropolitan Museum of Art, New York. Alfred Stieglitz Collection, 1933.

Alfred Stieglitz (1864–1946) was a photographer as well as a gallery director and editor. As a photographer he was recognized for the freshness and originality of his vision. As an editor of photography magazines, he supported the work of other innovative photographers. In Gallery 261, which he established with Edward Steichen, he exhibited the newest and most radical examples of modern painting, architecture, and sculpture.

A pioneer of modern art, Stieglitz championed the cause of photography as the first new art form to come along in five thousand years. His own photographs were straightforward and evoked strong emotional responses.

Stieglitz was married to painter Georgia O'Keeffe. The many photographs he took of her over the years are considered to be the most comprehensive portrait ever done of one person.

CHARLES E. BURCHFIELD.
November Evening. 1934.
Oil on canvas, 32⅛ × 52″.
The Metropolitan Museum of Art,
New York.
George A. Hearn Fund, 1934.

Charles Burchfield (1893–1967), born in Ohio and educated at Cleveland School of Art, painted scenes typical of rural America and filled them with fantasy and drama. His work is admired for the way it expresses personal feelings and the tremendous power of nature. Burchfield said about *November Evening*: "I have tried to express the coming of winter over the middle-west as it must have felt to the pioneers—great black clouds sweep out of the west at twilight as if to overwhelm not only the pitiful attempt at a town, but also the earth itself."

The dark clouds, the emptiness of the town, the posture of the man and horses combine to give a sense of loneliness and isolation.

ALEXANDER CALDER. *Slanting Red Nose.* 1969.
Gouache, 29½ × 43¼".
Collection, The Museum of Modern Art, New York.
Gift of Mr. and Mrs. Klaus G. Perls.

Alexander Calder was born in 1898 in Philadelphia and died in 1976. His father and grandfather were both sculptors, and he too is known more for his three-dimensional works than for his paintings. Calder is most famous for inventing delicately balanced sculptures that are held together by wires and move by air currents; the artist Marcel Duchamp named them "mobiles." Because they are constantly moving, these mobiles look different from moment to moment; exactly what the viewer sees as the "finished" sculpture depends on chance. Calder's use of chance as an element in sculpture influenced many other artists who followed him.

  Both his paintings and sculptures give a sense of exuberance, fantasy, and joy. Calder preferred pure reds, yellows, and blues—the primary colors—and used them with great humor and simplicity, as in this painting, *Slanting Red Nose.*

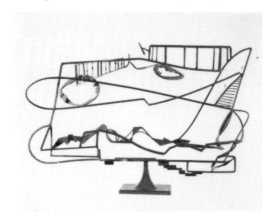

DAVID SMITH. *Hudson River Landscape.* 1951.
Steel, 49¼ × 75 × 16¾".
Collection of The Whitney Museum of American Art, New York.
Photograph by Jerry L. Thompson.

David Smith (1906–1965) began as a Cubist painter earning his living as a metal worker, and eventually turned to sculpture. He described the transition by saying: "The painting developed into raised levels from the canvas. Gradually the canvas was the base and the painting was a sculpture." He was greatly influenced by the works of Spanish sculptor Julio González and Pablo Picasso.

  Hudson River Landscape is an example of "drawing in space." It was the first piece of open sculpture in the modern era and was intended to be viewed from the front only. Smith had no preconceived plan for it; the sculpture came to him spontaneously as he worked on it.

  Considered to be one of the most important twentieth-century sculptors, Smith was the first in America to weld in iron. He produced many works and brought a fresh, typically American vision and industrial skill to the formal, more European concepts of sculpture. He expressed his love for technology by saying: "The equipment I use, my supply of material comes from factory study, and duplicates as nearly as possible the production equipment used in making a locomotive. . . . What associations the metal possesses are those of this century: power, structure, movement, progress, suspension, destruction, brutality."

CONRAD MARCA-RELLI. *Junction.* 1958.
Collage of painted canvas, 56 × 77¼″.
Collection of The Whitney Museum of American Art,
New York.
Gift of the Friends of The Whitney Museum
of American Art.
Photograph by Geoffrey Clements Photography.

Junction is a collage by Conrad Marca-Relli (1913–   ), who specializes in combining oil paint and collage in a large format. Born in Boston and mostly self-taught in painting technique, Marca-Relli frequently begins his work with the suggestion of a human figure, then pastes canvas scraps to the background and covers them with painted brushstrokes. The completed work is abstract, marked by free expression, and often done on a monumental scale. He is considered to be an American master of collage.

NIKI DE SAINT PHALLE. *Black Venus.* 1967.
Painted polyester, 110″ × 35″ × 24″.
Collection of The Whitney Museum of American Art, New York.
Gift of the Howard and Jean Lipman Foundation.

Niki de Saint Phalle (1930–   ) is a "pop" artist born in New York City and is now living in France. She is known for her zany and humorous "Nanas"—large, exaggerated sculptures of women with tiny heads, featureless faces, targets, hearts, and flowers decorating the huge bodies. By emphasizing the body instead of the head, the artist makes amusing comment on stereotypes of women.

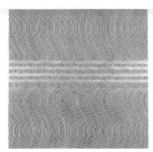

BRIDGET RILEY. *Current.* 1964.
Synthetic polymer paint on composition board,
58⅜ × 38⅞″.
Collection, The Museum of Modern Art, New York.
Philip Johnson Fund.

Op Art is a kind of dynamic, graphic design that depends on visual devices and optical illusions. It became popular during the late 1960s after a major exhibit titled The Responsive Eye was held in 1965 at New York's Museum of Modern Art.

Unlike some other Op artists who have been accused of merely painting visual tricks, Bridget Riley (1931–   ) has consistently produced works of depth. An English member of the Op Art movement, she uses optical effects to express facets of her own personality and to interpret her impressions of natural landscapes. *Current* is an abstract interpretation of the pattern ripples make on a stream. Its close black-and-white wave pattern hits the viewer's eyes with movement and is typical of the black-and-white work she painted exclusively from 1960 to 1967.